# PRICE ACTION STRATEGIES

A BEGINNER'S GUIDE TO PROFITABLE TRADING TECHNIQUES

JAMES WILLY

Copyright © 2024 James Willy

All rights reserved.

# TABLE OF CONTENT

## INTRODUCTION — 7

**The Journey to Price Action Trading** — 7

## CHAPTER 1 — 13

**Understanding The Foundation** — 13
- Power of Pure Price Action — 13
- What is price action trading — 14
- Why does price action trading work — 15
- The Psychology of Price Movement — 16
- Important Tools for Price Action Trading — 17
- Setting up your charts for success — 17
- The three pillars of price action — 18

## CHAPTER 2 — 21

**The Language of Price** — 21
- Understanding Candlestick Patterns — 21
- The Story Behind Each Candle — 22
- Key Components of Price Movement — 23
- Market Structure: Peaks, Lows, and Trends — 24
- Volume and its Relationship to Price — 25
- Reading Between The Lines — 26
- Importance of Timeframes — 26

| False signals and true patterns | 27 |

## CHAPTER 3    29

**Market Psychology and Pricing Behaviour**    29

| Understanding the Market Phases | 29 |
| The role of various market participants | 30 |
| Reading Market Sentiment | 31 |
| Common Price Action Traps | 32 |
| Smart Money against Retail Traders | 32 |
| Psychology of Support and Resistance | 34 |
| Fear, Greed and Market Movements | 35 |
| Time and Price Relationships | 35 |
| Mastering Market Psychology | 36 |

## CHAPTER 4    39

**Core Price Action Strategies**    39

| Pin-Bar Trading Strategy | 39 |
| Inside Bar Strategy | 41 |
| Engulfing Pattern Strategy | 43 |
| Multiple Time Frame Analysis | 45 |
| The Power of Round Numbers | 46 |
| Find High-Probability Setups | 47 |
| Timing your entries | 47 |
| Manage Your Exits | 48 |
| Risk Management Integration | 49 |

## CHAPTER 5 — 51

**Advanced Price Action Concepts** — 51
- Price Action at Key Levels — 51
- Swing Trading and Price Action — 52
- Breakout Trading Strategies — 53
- Reversal Patterns and Setups — 55
- Continuation patterns — 59
- Complex Pattern Recognition — 63

## CHAPTER 6 — 65

**Trade Management and Risk Control** — 65
- Position Sizing Principles — 65
- Setting Strategic Stop Losses — 66
- Managing Running Trades — 67
- Scaling In and Out of Position — 68
- Risk-Reward Optimisation — 69
- Dynamic Position Management — 69
- The Psychology Of Trade Management — 70
- Risk Management Evolution — 71

## CHAPTER 7 — 73

**Market Context and Trading Environment** — 73
- Trading under Various Market Conditions — 73
- Price Action in Trending Markets. — 74
- Range-Bound Market Strategies — 75

| | |
|---|---|
| Volatile Market Approaches | 75 |
| News Impact on Price Action | 76 |
| Session-Based Trading Opportunities | 77 |
| Market Depth and Price Action | 78 |
| Seasonal Market Patterns | 79 |
| Correlation Effects | 79 |
| Adapting to Market Change | 80 |

## CHAPTER 8 — 83

**Developing Your Trading Plan — 83**

| | |
|---|---|
| Developing a Strategy Blueprint | 83 |
| Creating Your Trading Routine | 84 |
| Record-keeping and Trade Journal | 85 |
| Performance Analysis | 85 |
| Common Mistakes To Avoid | 86 |
| Psychology & Discipline | 87 |
| Strategy Testing and Validation | 88 |
| Adapting to Market Change | 88 |
| Risk Management Framework | 89 |
| The Road to Consistency | 90 |

## CHAPTER 9 — 93

**Advanced Price Action Mastery — 93**

| | |
|---|---|
| Combining Multiple Patterns | 93 |
| Complex price action setups | 94 |
| Order Flow Analysis | 95 |

| | |
|---|---|
| Institutional Trading Levels | 95 |
| Advanced Entry Techniques | 96 |
| Pattern Evolution and Adaptation | 98 |
| Advanced Risk Management | 98 |
| Market microstructure analysis | 99 |
| The Path of Mastery | 100 |

## CHAPTER 10 — 101

**Real-World Applications** — 101

| | |
|---|---|
| Live Trading Examples | 101 |
| Case Studies for Successful Trades | 102 |
| Common Scenarios and Solutions | 103 |
| Adapting to Market Change | 103 |
| Building Long-Term Consistency | 104 |
| Creating Your Trading Edge | 105 |
| Real Market Challenges | 106 |
| Risk Management in Practice | 106 |
| The Journey to Proficiency | 107 |

## CONCLUSION — 109

# Introduction

## The Journey to Price Action Trading

Trading transformed my life in ways I never expected. Back in 2008, I peered at charts filled with various indicators, including moving averages, RSI, MACD, and what felt like a rainbow of overlapping lines. Like many newbies, I believed that more indicators meant better trading judgements. I was totally wrong.

You are undoubtedly curious as to why I am sharing this with you. My journey from an indicator-dependent trader to a price action specialist is similar to that of many traders. The day I stripped my charts bare, leaving simply raw price movement, was the start of my professional trading career.

Price action trading is more than just a strategy; it is the foundation of all market analysis. It is what the largest banks and institutional traders utilise. They do not use lagging indicators; instead, they read the market's basic language. Through this book, I'll show you how to do it.

Allow me to tell you about my first pure price action trade. The market was EUR/USD, and after removing all indicators, I felt exposed and vulnerable. But, for the first time, I understood what was going on. A clear rejection at an important level, followed by a rapid bearish move. That single trade yielded more profit than my prior month of indicator-based trading. More importantly, it felt different: I knew exactly why I made the trade.

But please do not misunderstand me. Price action trading is not a get-rich-quick program. It takes commitment, patience, and a willingness to perceive the market for what it truly is: a reflection of mass psychology.

Over the years of trading and training others, I've witnessed both stunning successes and devastating disappointments. Understanding the guiding ideas we'll cover in this book is frequently the deciding factor.

You might wonder, "Why should I trust price action over indicators?" It is a valid question. Indicators have their place, but it's like watching a movie with subtitles that arrive 20 seconds later. Price action allows you to comprehend the story as it unfolds. When you learn to interpret price action, you are reading the market's original language, not a translation.

In my trading room, I've seen several "aha" moments where traders suddenly understand price action ideas. One learner, who had been struggling with sophisticated indicator systems for years, nearly burst into tears after completing her first successful week using only price action.

**You'll learn how to:**

- Interpret market behaviour based solely on price movement in this book.

- Identify high-probability trading opportunities.

- Develop a confident, independent trading approach

- Effective risk management

- Create long-term trading plans

Each chapter builds on the preceding one, resulting in a complete trading strategy. We'll start with the basics, but don't fear; even experienced traders frequently discover fresh insights in fundamental ideas. I'll post actual trades, both winners and failures, because that's how we really learn.

Before we go any further, let's clarify that price action trading isn't about predicting the future. It is all about understanding market behaviour and likelihood.

In my fifteen years of trading, I've learnt that successful trading is more about risk management and understanding market psychology than finding the right setup.

Remember Sarah? She was one of my first students. She had a background in physics and wanted everything to be precisely perfect. Something clicked after three months of struggling with price action. "Trading isn't about being right," she advised me; "it's about being profitable." She now manages a large portfolio mostly using price action tactics.

Throughout this book, I will break down difficult ideas into manageable chunks. You'll learn through real-world examples, practical applications, and lessons gleaned from genuine market experience. Some thoughts may question your present trading beliefs, which is fine. Questioning what we believe we know is a common catalyst for growth.

The journey ahead involves more than just understanding trading tactics. It is about gaining a better understanding of market behaviour and, maybe more crucially, your own trading psyche. By the end of this book, you'll have the tools and knowledge to trade with confidence, reading the market's language without the distraction of too many indicators.

Are you ready to start this journey? Let's start by understanding price action and why it is the foundation of effective trading.

# Chapter 1

## Understanding The Foundation

**Power of Pure Price Action**

Price action trading is the oldest and most fundamental method of market analysis. It reads basic market movements, free of indicators and sophisticated algorithms. In my early trading days, I became infatuated with every technical indicator available, believing they held the key to constant earnings. After years of mixed results, I realised that the true power was in understanding pure price movement.

## What is price action trading?

Price action trading is the analysis and execution of trades based entirely on price movements. It entails studying how prices react at specific levels, identifying patterns in market movement, and making trading decisions based on these findings. Unlike indicator-based trading, price action provides real-time market data without the lag associated with calculated indicators.

During my years heading a trading desk in Singapore, I saw that the most successful traders rarely employed indicators. Price movement, support and resistance levels, and market structure were all areas of significant focus. These traders consistently outperformed their peers, who relied mainly on technical indicators.

## Why does price action trading work?

The efficiency of price action trading originates from its direct relationship to market psychology. Each price movement reflects the combined decisions of all market participants. When you learn to read price action, you are essentially studying market psychology.

I recall one EUR/USD trade in which the price had been dropping for hours. Most indicators pointed to continuing selling, but price action told a different story. Small bodied candles with long wicks indicated that selling pressure was weakening. Taking a contrarian position based solely on price action resulted in substantial profits when the market abruptly turned.

## The Psychology of Price Movement

Every single tick in the forex market is driven by market psychology. Fear, greed, and uncertainty generate patterns that are consistent across all timeframes. Understanding these patterns offers you a huge advantage in anticipating future market trends.

Trading the GBPJPY throughout the Brexit negotiations taught me important lessons about market psychology. The high price jumps and steep retracements accurately mirrored the market's emotional condition throughout each news announcement. Pure price action guided me through this turbulence considerably more effectively than any indicator could.

## Important Tools for Price Action Trading

The beauty of price action trading is in its simplicity. To efficiently trade, you only need a few tools:

A clear price chart with candlesticks or bars.

Horizontal lines to show support and resistance.

A method for measuring price movement.

Basic Trend Lines

That is it. There's no need for elaborate indicators or advanced algorithms. This simplicity allows you to focus solely on price behaviour rather than handling many indicators.

**Setting up your charts for success.**

In price action trading, chart setup is essential. Through years of experimentation, I discovered that simplicity leads to clarity.

Begin with a clean chart with candlesticks or bars. Draw a couple horizontal lines to indicate key support and resistance levels. Keep your charts clutter-free to see price action clearly.

When I advise new traders, the first thing we do is take all indicators off their charts. Many people initially resist, feeling vulnerable without their regular tools. However, within weeks, the majority report a better understanding of market fluctuations and increased trading performance.

## The three pillars of price action

Price action trading is based on three core principles: trend recognition, support and resistance levels, and candlestick patterns. These components work together to create a comprehensive trading system.

The greatest profitable trade I ever made was based exclusively on these three pillars. During the 2015 Swiss Franc shock, when most traders panicked, unambiguous price action signs helped me locate a high-probability trading opportunity. The market had established a firm support level, demonstrated a defined trend, and provided precise entry indications via candlestick patterns.

This chapter taught you the fundamentals of price action trading. Understanding the fundamentals is critical before progressing to more advanced concepts. In the following chapter, we will look at how to read individual candlesticks and grasp the story they convey about market emotion.

Remember that mastering price action trading requires time and experience. The concepts may appear easy, but their implementation necessitates patience and attention.

Before proceeding, ensure that you have a solid understanding of each idea. Your success in price action trading will be based on these fundamental fundamentals.

# Chapter 2

## The Language of Price

**Understanding Candlestick Patterns**

More so than any indication, price movement alone conveys a tale. Throughout my fifteen years of trading experience, I've discovered that candlestick patterns serve as the market's native language. Each candlestick represents a conflict between buyers and sellers, showing who won the fight.

During my time trading in Tokyo, I worked with traders who had perfected the technique of candlestick analysis.

They taught me that each candlestick contains four critical pieces of information: open, high, low, and close. The relationship between these points shows market sentiment during that time period.

**The Story Behind Each Candle.**

The body of a candlestick indicates who won the period, whether buyers or sellers. lengthy bullish candles imply significant buying pressure, whilst lengthy bearish candles signal overwhelming selling. The wicks, or shadows, reveal the entire range of price movement over that time period.

I once saw a superb example of trading USD/JPY. Following a decline, a long-bodied bullish candle appeared, with tiny wicks at each end. This demonstrated that buyers took control from the open and maintained pressure until the close. Taking a long position based on a single candle pattern resulted in one of my most profitable trades that month.

## Key Components of Price Movement:

Price movement has three basic components: trend, momentum, and volatility. The trend depicts the overall direction, momentum represents the strength of movement, and volatility displays the market's emotional state.

Trading EURUSD after key ECB statements has taught me how these components interact. High volatility leads to wider candle ranges, whereas strong momentum creates candles with few wicks in the trend direction (Support and Resistance: The Building Blocks).

The foundation of price action trading is support and resistance levels. These levels are notoriously difficult for price to break through. My greatest effective trades have frequently resulted from observing price behaviour at these important levels.

In 2019, I saw that the GBPUSD consistently failed to break above 1.3200. Each attempt resulted in smaller-bodied candles with longer higher wicks, indicating a weaker buying pressure. This pattern resulted in a strong downward move, demonstrating once again how price action at critical levels can foretell future movements.

## Market Structure: Peaks, Lows, and Trends

The market structure offers context for all price action analysis. If the highs and lows are both higher, then the trend is upwards; if they are both lower, then the trend is downwards. Understanding this structure aids in predicting potential price movements.

One noteworthy trade saw the AUDUSD record a series of lower highs during what appeared to be a consolidation phase.

The market structure suggested weakness long before the huge drop, allowing me to position myself ahead of the trend.

## Volume and its Relationship to Price

While forex does not have direct volume data like stock markets, price action can reveal underlying volume by candle size and movement patterns. Large candles with strong closures typically imply great volume and conviction in the move.

Trading USDJPY throughout Asian sessions taught me how volume influences price action. Smaller candles with longer wicks were more common during low-volume periods, whereas stronger, more definitive moves occurred after Tokyo opened and volume soared.

## Reading Between The Lines

The tiny nuances in price action frequently reveal patterns that are not immediately visible. Small dojis after large moves may indicate weariness. Clusters of small-bodied candles may suggest accumulation or distribution. These tiny signals become obvious after spending enough time observing pure price action.

During the 2020 market turbulence, these small signals were crucial. While others relied on trailing indications, monitoring pure price action allowed me to detect probable reversal moments and retain profitability in the face of severe volatility.

## Importance of Timeframes

Different time periods tell different stories, but price action principles are consistent across them all.

I trade mostly on the 4-hour and daily charts since I believe these time frames deliver the clearest signals with the least noise.

A bearish pattern on the daily chart was supported by similar patterns on the 4-hour time frame in a trading setup that demonstrated this argument. This multi-time frame confirmation utilising just price action resulted in one of my top reward-to-risk trades of the year.

**False signals and true patterns.**

Not all price action signals result in a profitable trade. Experience helps you discern between false signals and reliable patterns. The goal is to understand context and confirm signals across multiple time frames.

The information presented in this chapter lays the groundwork for more sophisticated price action techniques.

In the following chapter, we'll look at how market psychology shapes these patterns and generates trading opportunities.

Your journey into price action trading will demand patience and persistent observation. With practice, the patterns and principles outlined here will become second nature to you, allowing you to fluently understand the market language.

# Chapter 3

## Market Psychology and Pricing Behaviour

**Understanding the Market Phases**

Markets go through several phases, each reflecting the collective psychology of traders. Throughout my years managing institutional trades, I've noticed that these periods occur regularly across all currency pairs. The accumulation phase demonstrates modest purchase by clever money. Distribution reflects cautious selling by major players. Mark-up and mark-down phases demonstrate the clear trends that most retail traders seek.

Working at a major FX desk in London showed me how these phases occur in real time. I witnessed major institutions discreetly accumulate positions before prices surged in the expected way. They understood mass psychology and harnessed it to their benefit.

## The role of various market participants

Every market move is the result of interactions between various types of traders. Banks, hedge funds, retail traders, and algorithmic systems all play a role. Each group behaves differently, resulting in predictable price action patterns.

During my time trading institutional money, I noticed how large orders influenced market behaviour. A major bank may split a huge buy order into smaller pieces, resulting in a succession of subtle bullish price patterns that most retail traders overlook. Understanding these patterns provided me an advantage when anticipating short-term market trends.

## Reading Market Sentiment

Market mood fluctuates between fear and greed, resulting in distinct price patterns. Strong trends can end with extreme optimism or pessimism. I've learnt to identify these emotional extremes by plain price action.

Trading GBPUSD throughout the Brexit negotiations provided excellent evidence of emotion changes. Panic selling created long-wicked candles at support levels, providing ideal buying opportunities for those who could read the market's emotional state.

## Common Price Action Traps

The market frequently creates traps for uninformed traders. False breakouts, stop hunts, and liquidity grabs generate repeatable patterns across all periods. I fell into similar traps early in my career, but I now see them as trading opportunities.

One noteworthy trade was a false breach below a major support level in the EURUSD. Most traders panicked and sold, but the price action followed conventional trap patterns. Taking a contrarian long strategy resulted in big profits when the market turned abruptly.

## Smart Money against Retail Traders

Smart money (banks and institutions) operates differently than retail traders.

They slowly accumulate and disperse positions. Understanding their behaviour patterns through price action provides a big benefit.

In my trading room, I frequently discuss how smart money leaves indications in price action. Subtle resistance tests, false breaks, and quiet accumulation periods frequently precede major advances. These patterns become obvious once you know what to look for.

How Banks and Institutions Influence The Market

Large financial firms do not trade in the same way that retail traders do. They cannot enter or exit positions fast without impacting the price. Their actions produce distinct price patterns that indicate their goals.

During my institutional trading days, I observed how huge orders were executed in the market.

A billion-dollar position might take days to establish, resulting in unique price patterns along the way. These patterns now form the foundation of my trading technique.

## Psychology of Support and Resistance

Price moves differently at major levels because traders react collectively to them. Through years of study, I've noticed how mass psychology causes support and resistance levels to become self-fulfilling prophecies.

Trading USDJPY taught me how past highs and lows influence trader behaviour. When prices reached these levels, little variations in candlestick patterns frequently indicated whether a break or reversal was more likely.

## Fear, Greed and Market Movements

Price action is motivated by human emotions. Fear causes sharp, volatile movements with lengthy wicks. Greed causes powerful trending movements with little wicks. Learning to recognise these emotional characteristics in price action greatly enhances trading judgements.

After learning to trade despite intense emotions, I had my most profitable period. When others panicked during the 2015 Swiss Franc incident, reading price action allowed me to remain objective and locate lucrative trades amidst pandemonium.

## Time and Price Relationships

Different times of day induce distinct price action patterns.

The overlap between major trading sessions frequently results in unusual price behaviour. Understanding these time patterns provides an additional layer to price action analysis.

Trading from Asia taught me how price action varies throughout the worldwide trading day. The modest patterns observed during Asian hours frequently provided hints about expected moves during London and New York sessions.

## Mastering Market Psychology

Understanding technical patterns and market psychology is necessary for successful price action trading. The finest trades occur when technical and psychological aspects align. Through years of trading, I've discovered that psychology frequently outperforms technical analysis.

The concepts in this chapter provide the foundation for understanding advanced price action patterns. In the following chapter, we will look at specific trading methods based on these psychological principles. Remember that the market's psychology never changes, thus these patterns are consistently tradeable across all timeframes.

Understanding these psychological factors is critical to your growth as a price action trader. They add meaning to every technological pattern and help explain why some arrangements function better than others.

# Chapter 4

## Core Price Action Strategies

**Pin-Bar Trading Strategy**

The pin bar pattern is regarded as one of the most significant price action signs. Throughout my decade of trading, I've discovered that pin bars are very helpful at important support and resistance levels. These candles, distinguished by their long wicks and short bodies, indicate a strong rejection of specific price levels.

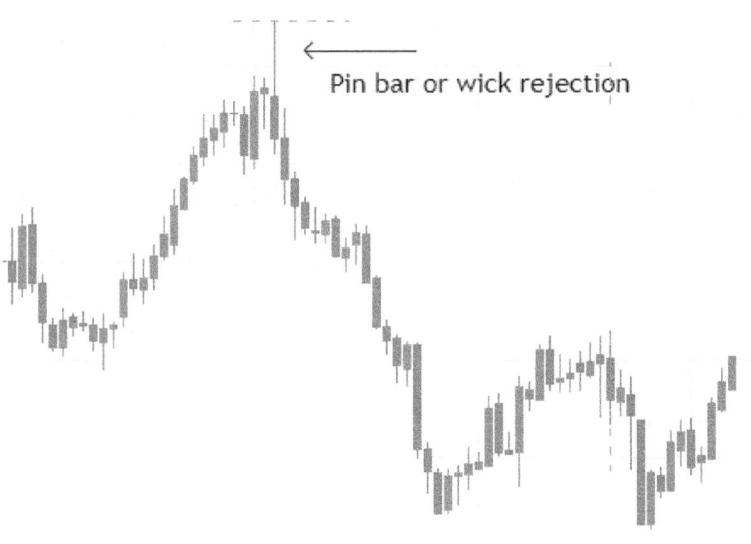

Trading USDJPY in 2019, I noticed a fantastic pin bar at a big resistance level.

The extended upper wick demonstrated a strong rejection of rising prices, while the little bearish body indicated that sellers had won the war. Taking a short trade based on this single pattern resulted in a 200-pip profit within 48 hours.

**Inside Bar Strategy**

Inside bars indicate periods of consolidation, which frequently precede big moves. My institutional trading expertise has taught me that these patterns often develop when smart money acquires holdings. The idea is to recognise within bars that appear following strong trending moves.

A very good trade occurred on the GBPUSD when three consecutive inside bars formed following a strong rally. The compression of price action indicated increasing pressure. When price finally broke above the mother bar's high, the subsequent move generated 180 pips of pure profit.

## Engulfing Pattern Strategy

Engulfing patterns have a specific significance in price action trading. A well-formed engulfing candle represents one side of the market dominating the other. Through countless trades, I've learnt that the context of these patterns is more important than the pattern itself.

During the EUR crisis, I identified a huge move utilising an engulfing pattern. Following several weeks of fall, a huge bullish engulfing candle emerged at a major support level. The firm rejection of lower prices, paired with the pattern's placement, resulted in a high-probability trade opportunity.

## Multiple Time Frame Analysis

Combining price action analysis over many time frames improves trading accuracy dramatically. My trading strategy normally begins with daily charts to identify trends, then progresses to 4-hour and 1-hour charts to choose entry points.

A prime example occurred while trading AUDUSD. The daily chart demonstrated an obvious downturn, while the 4-hour chart displayed a flawless pin bar near resistance. This multi-timeframe confluence resulted in a high-probability short trade for 150 pips.

## The Power of Round Numbers

Price reacts heavily near round figures such as 1.3000 or 0.7500. These levels frequently form psychological obstacles when traders make decisions. My years in institutional trading taught me that these levels usually attract significant orders.

Trading EURUSD at 1.2000 level presented various options. As major players defended or challenged this psychological barrier, the price action around this level frequently formed dependable patterns. Understanding this behaviour resulted in multiple profitable trades.

## Find High-Probability Setups

When numerous elements align, high-probability situations develop. Through years of trading, I've established three crucial elements: trend direction, key level confluence, and a clear price action indicator. When these three factors align, the likelihood of a successful trade skyrockets.

My most profitable trade in 2020 contained all of these elements. The GBPJPY displayed a strong advance on the daily chart, approached a big resistance level, and produced a bearish engulfing pattern on the 4-hour period. This system enabled a 300-pip move in days.

## Timing your entries.

Entry timing frequently influences trade outcome. Price action gives precise entry signals based on distinct candle closes. I've learnt to wait for a full candle formation before joining trades to avoid the trap of hasty entry.

Trading USD/CAD taught me to be patient with entry execution. A promising pin bar configuration once enticed me to enter before the candle went out. The final candle shape shifted considerably throughout the last several minutes, showing me the value of waiting for confirmation.

## Manage Your Exits

Exit tactics are as important as entry. Price action sends obvious signs for both partial and full departures. Through experience, I've learnt to exit positions utilising price action cues rather than fixed targets.

This method was proven in a noteworthy EURGBP trade. Following a strong advance, bearish price action at resistance caused me to take some profits. This decision preserved benefits when the market subsequently turned.

## Risk Management Integration

Each price action approach necessitates effective risk management. Instead of using preset pip levels, I use stops that are positioned beyond significant price action points. This strategy has saved my money numerous times amid unforeseen market fluctuations.

During volatile market conditions, this strategy proved invaluable. Trading USDCHF during an SNB announcement, I kept my stop above a critical price action level, preventing a hasty exit despite high volatility.

The ideas presented in this chapter lay the groundwork for profitable price action trading. In the following chapter, we will look at more sophisticated notions that build on these foundational principles. Your success is dependent on learning these fundamentals before progressing to more sophisticated arrangements.

Remember that any technique takes time to master and must be tailored to your specific trading style. All markets and timeframes can use the patterns, but your execution must align with your risk tolerance and trading objectives.

# Chapter 5

## Advanced Price Action Concepts

**Price Action at Key Levels**

Key levels in forex markets operate as price magnets, providing unique trading possibilities. Through my institutional trading experience, I've seen how prices react differently at these critical times. The combination between price and these levels frequently yields solid trading setups.

Trading EURUSD at big levels taught me the value of patience. At 1.2000, price frequently developed intricate patterns before executing its next major move. Small rejections and false breaks sometimes preceded a true breakout or reversal.

These minor hints, evident only through pure price action, proved crucial in timing entrances.

## Swing Trading and Price Action

Swing trading with price action necessitates a better understanding of market structure. The best swing trades emerge when numerous timing analyses corroborate a potential movement. My trading record demonstrates that capturing large swings needs accurate assessment of both price action and market context.

One of my most winning swing trades was in GBPJPY. The daily chart showed a series of higher lows while the price consolidated near resistance. The four-hour chart demonstrated accumulation using minor price action patterns. When the price ultimately broke higher, the advance continued for several days.

## Breakout Trading Strategies.

True breakouts have unique price action features that set them apart from false breaks. Years of trading have taught me that genuine breakouts exhibit strong momentum candles with minimal wicks in the breakout direction. The quality of the breakout frequently dictates the power of the next move.

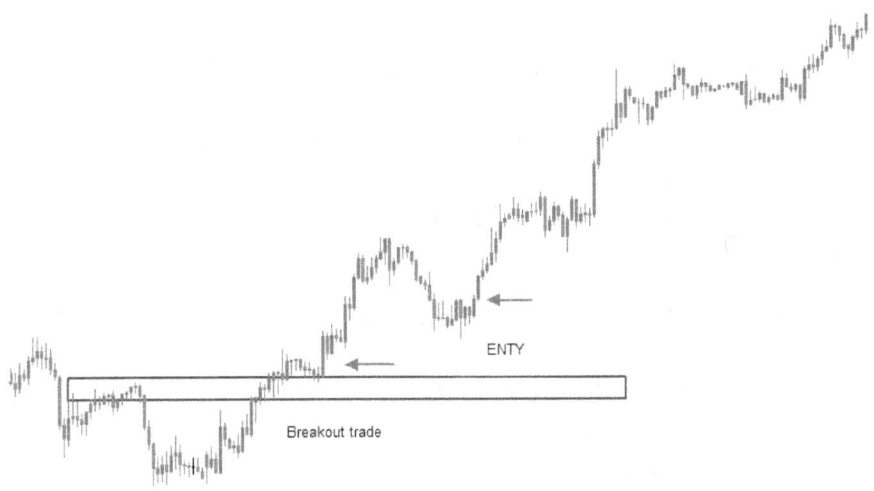

A USDCAD breakout trade jumps out in my mind. After weeks of consolidation, price broke through resistance with a strong bullish candle. The lack of upper wick and strong closure indicated serious buying pressure. This setup resulted in 250 pips over the next three sessions, using false break patterns.

When false breaks are correctly spotted, they provide fantastic trading opportunities. These patterns trap traders on the wrong side of the market, leading to abrupt market reversals. In my experience, false breaks frequently occur at major psychological levels.

Trading AUDUSD presented an excellent illustration. The price briefly fell below 0.7000, resulting in a large number of sell orders. However, the price action demonstrated weakness in the downward trend with long lower wicks. Taking a contrarian long position following the false break yielded significant profits.

**Reversal Patterns and Setups**

Reversal patterns need accurate identification and timing. Through years of trading, I've learnt that the biggest reversals occur when price action reversal indications coincide with important support or resistance levels.

Double top

Double bottom

# Head and shoulder pattern

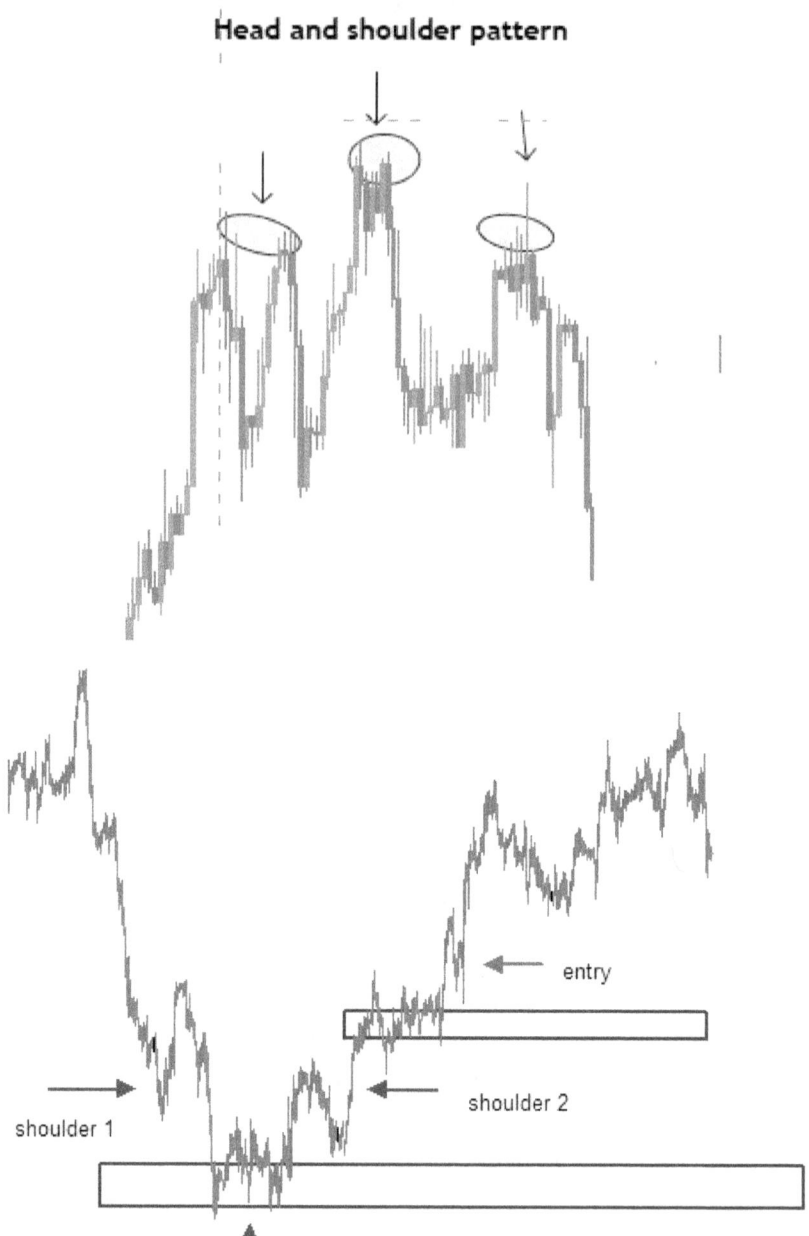

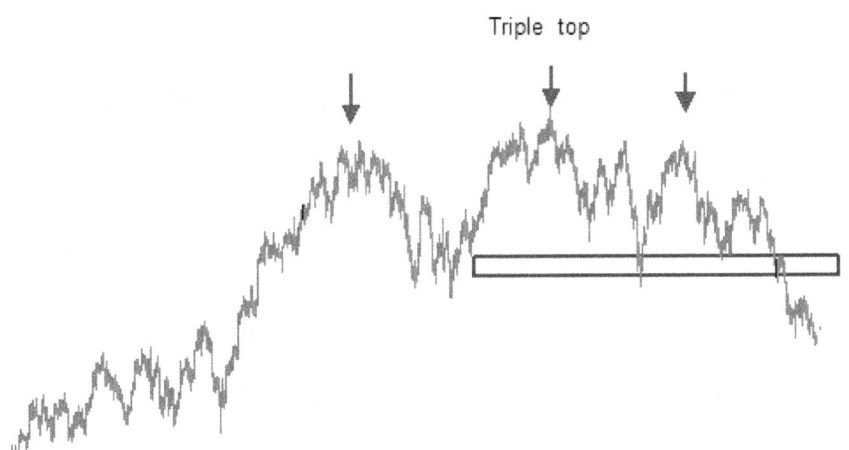

During the 2018 USDJPY drop, I noticed a reversal pattern that incorporated several price action cues. A series of diminishing bearish candles emerged at support, which was followed by a strong bullish engulfing pattern. This combination marked the conclusion of the downtrend and the start of a major rally.

## Continuation patterns

Continuation patterns provide lower-risk entrances into established trends. My trading journal reveals that the most consistent continuation setups emerge following healthy pullbacks to crucial levels. Price action during these pullbacks frequently exposes the underlying trend's strength.

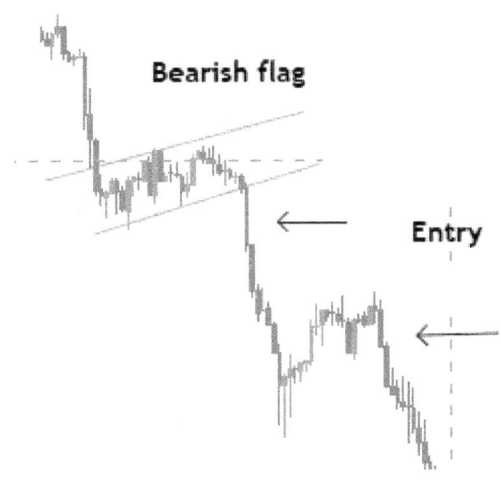

One remarkable EURUSD trade used a continuation pattern during a strong rise. Price returned to previous resistance turned support, resulting in three small-bodied candles. These wicks' lack of downward momentum indicated that the downturn had stopped, leading to a profitable long entry.

Advanced Entry Techniques.

Refined entry tactics greatly improve trading timeliness. Instead of making trades as soon as patterns appear, I've devised ways for entering trades based on price action in lower time frames. This strategy frequently improves entry prices while maintaining the overall pattern's validity.

Trading GBPUSD showed me the importance of accurate entry. Rather than entering a daily pin bar setup right away, using hourly price action to fine-tune entry resulted in improved risk-reward ratios and higher probability trades.

## Complex Pattern Recognition

Complex patterns integrate several price action elements. I've learnt from experience that these patterns frequently produce the highest probability configurations. The key is to understand how the various price action factors interact.

A complex pattern in NZDUSD included an inside bar formation, a false break, and a reversal. Understanding how these components interacted resulted in one of my most lucrative trades of the quarter. The pattern's complexity repelled many traders, resulting in less competition at the entry point.

The principles discussed in this chapter build on the groundwork built previously. In the following chapter, we'll look at how to manage these sophisticated settings effectively. Success with these patterns necessitates repetition and meticulous attention to detail.

Mastering these advanced ideas promotes your development as a price action trader. They offer extra techniques for spotting high-probability trades while successfully minimising risk.

# Chapter 6

## Trade Management and Risk Control

**Position Sizing Principles**

Position sizing is the cornerstone of effective trading. During my years of managing institutional funds, I discovered that even the best price action setups fail without proper position sizing. Your account's survival is determined more by how much you risk than by your win rate.

During my early trading days in London, I saw brilliant traders squander their funds due to overleveraging, while having good research skills.

The market taught me that risking 1-2% per trade achieves the best blend of development potential and account protection.

**Setting Strategic Stop Losses.**

Stop loss placement needs both art and science. Price action creates natural stop points, which are generally located beyond key swing points or pattern extremes. My experience suggests that stops placed at visible levels are frequently activated before the market moves in the desired direction.

Trading EURUSD during volatile sessions offered me significant skills in stop placement. Placing stops beyond the previous swing high, rather than utilising a predetermined pip distance, rescued my positions several times when the price spiked before continuing its trend.

Profit-taking strategies greatly effect total profitability. Through years of trading, I've built a hybrid strategy that combines price action signals with predetermined targets. The market frequently displays weariness indications near important levels, indicating natural exit points.

One especially lucrative GBPJPY trade exemplified this strategy brilliantly. Following a powerful upward advance, I noted bearish price action developing at a key resistance level. Taking partial profits maintained profits while allowing the balance to run generated extra upside.

## Managing Running Trades

Active trade management frequently affects eventual profitability. Your position requires different treatment based on whether it shows a profit or loss. My trading records demonstrate that competent trade management frequently converts moderate winners into big profits.

Trading USDCAD has taught me the value of active management. Because I altered my stop loss depending on emergent price action patterns rather than sticking to a fixed plan, a trade that started with small returns finally yielded triple the initial aim.

## Scaling In and Out of Position

Strategic scaling maximises lucrative trades while minimising risk. My institutional expertise shown that huge positions could be formed or reduced without materially affecting market price. The goal is to identify the appropriate moments for increasing or lowering exposure.

During a strong AUDUSD trend, I scaled into positions on pullbacks with favourable price action. Each additional position had its own stop loss, resulting in a pyramid structure that maximised profit possibilities while keeping risk levels manageable.

## Risk-Reward Optimisation

Optimal risk-reward ratios vary according to setup quality. Through considerable trading, I've discovered that greater probability setups can function with lower reward ratios, whereas lower probability trades require higher potential rewards to be profitable.

One noteworthy EURGBP trade provided a 5:1 reward-to-risk ratio at a key support level. Despite the lesser probability of the reversal setup, the favourable ratio made it a worthwhile trade, ultimately grabbing the entire goal.

## Dynamic Position Management.

Market conditions necessitate flexible position management.

Your strategy requires adjustment based on volatility and trend strength. My trading log shows that the most lucrative periods were from changing management style to market conditions.

Trading during the 2020 volatility spike requires entirely different management measures. Tighter stops and speedier profit-taking outperformed my regular longer-term holding strategy during those tumultuous sessions.

## The Psychology Of Trade Management

Managing open trades tests your psychological fortitude. Every trader experiences the impulse to take rapid profits or hold losing trades for too long. According to my experience, implementing pre-planned management principles can assist you overcome these emotional obstacles.

A USDJPY position tested my discipline when price moved strongly in my favor then retraced sharply. Sticking to my predetermined management plan, rather than panic selling, allowed the trade to eventually reach its full target.

## Risk Management Evolution

Your risk management approach must evolve with your trading journey. Starting with strict rules provides necessary discipline, but experience allows more flexible approaches based on market reading skills. My risk management has evolved significantly since my early trading days.

The concepts covered in this chapter protect your capital while maximizing profits. In the next chapter, we'll explore how different market conditions affect trading decisions. Success in forex trading requires both effective trade entry and skilled position management.

Your growth as a trader accelerates when you master these management principles. They provide the framework for consistent profitability while protecting your trading capital.

# Chapter 7

## Market Context and Trading Environment

**Trading under Various Market Conditions**

Markets move between trending, range, and volatile stages. Throughout my years of trading institutional money, I've seen how price action characteristics fluctuate substantially with market conditions. Recognising these developments early on provides you a considerable advantage when adapting your strategy.

In 2019, while trading EURUSD, the market moved from a strong trend to a narrow range.

The price action revealed unmistakable signs: momentum slowed, ranges narrowed, and reversals grew more common. I avoided a major drawdown by adapting my strategy early on.

## Price Action in Trending Markets.

Trending markets show distinct price action patterns. Strong trends favour larger-bodied candles with fewer wicks. My experience suggests that pullbacks during strong trends frequently result in the best trading opportunities.

Trading GBPUSD amid a strong rise taught me many good things. Each downturn produced smaller-bodied candles with longer wicks, indicating weak countertrend advances. These patterns made good starting points for entering the main trend.

## Range-Bound Market Strategies

Tactics for range markets differ from those for trending conditions. Price action at range borders frequently yields reliable trading indications. My trading history demonstrates that ranges produce predictable patterns at support and resistance levels.

During a three-month USDJPY range, I saw regular price action patterns at the boundaries. Strong rejection candles appeared at range extremes, indicating high-probability reversal trades. Understanding these patterns resulted in steady profitability despite minimal directional movement.

## Volatile Market Approaches

Volatile markets necessitate close attention to price action indications.

These periods are distinguished by large candles and swift reversals. Through trading many volatility spikes, I've learnt to modify position sizing and management approaches based on price action characteristics.

The 2020 market meltdown provided excellent examples of erratic price action. Large candles with lengthy wicks indicated considerable uncertainty. During these difficult conditions, I preserved my capital by reducing position sizes and waiting for unambiguous price action signs.

## News Impact on Price Action

Major news events result in distinct price action patterns. Price behaviour is frequently evident just before and just after news announcements. My institutional expertise taught me how to recognise these patterns for post-news trading opportunities.

Trading EURUSD during ECB statements produced consistent price action patterns. Pre-news consolidation followed by strong directional swings resulted in particular setups. Understanding these patterns enabled us to exploit post-news momentum while successfully managing risk.

## Session-Based Trading Opportunities

Different trading sessions have distinct price action characteristics. Asian sessions are frequently characterised by range behaviour, whereas London and New York sessions are distinguished by more directional moves. My trading in Tokyo showed me how session patterns influence price action.

USDJPY trading during Asian hours exhibited predictable patterns. Tight ranges with small-bodied candles usually preceded stronger changes during the London opening.

This understanding assisted in timed entries for maximum effectiveness.

## Market Depth and Price Action

Market depth determines price action patterns. Thin market conditions produce distinct price behaviour than liquid ones. Through years of institutional trading, I've learnt to tailor my strategy to market depth.

Trading AUDUSD during off-hours demonstrated how thin markets influence price action. Wider spreads and volatile volatility necessitated more conservative trading strategies. Understanding these conditions helped to avoid unwarranted losses during low liquidity periods.

## Seasonal Market Patterns

Markets exhibit seasonal patterns that influence price action. Holidays, month-end flows, and seasonal tendencies influence price behaviour. My trading journal demonstrates how these patterns repeat annually with surprising consistency.

December trading in major pairs educated me about end-of-year price action patterns. Reduced liquidity and institutional positioning resulted in distinct opportunities. Recognising these patterns aided profitability during traditionally difficult seasons.

## Correlation Effects

Correlated markets have an impact on each other's price actions. Understanding these links helps to confirm trading signals.

My experience has shown that strong moves frequently occur when numerous correlated pairs exhibit aligned price action.

Trading EURUSD while monitoring GBPUSD provided excellent insights. Similar price action patterns in both pairings frequently indicated stronger moves. This correlation awareness enhanced trade selection and timing.

## Adapting to Market Change

Markets continually change, necessitating strategy modification. Price action patterns that worked last month may require change today. Through decades of trading, I've learnt that adaptability and regular observation are essential for long-term success.

The concepts taught in this chapter will help you navigate various market conditions efficiently. The following chapter delves into how to create a complete trading strategy that incorporates these lessons. Your success is dependent on adapting your strategy to current market conditions.

# Chapter 8

## Developing Your Trading Plan

**Developing a Strategy Blueprint**

Professional traders can be distinguished from amateurs by having a sound trading plan. Throughout my experience managing institutional accounts, I've noticed that organised tactics consistently beat emotional trading. Your plan must cover all part of your trading operation, from analysis to execution.

During my time on the London trading floor, I seen competent traders fail simply because they had a solid plan.

A complete strategy blueprint has explicit entry criteria, risk parameters, and management procedures based only on price action signals.

## Creating Your Trading Routine

Successful trading necessitates consistent daily habits. My own practice begins with observing overnight price action across major pairings. I mark critical levels and probable setups every morning before the London session begins. This planning is critical for capturing early possibilities.

I learnt the importance of meticulous preparation while trading EURUSD. Following a rigid regimen allowed me to catch some significant moves that others missed due to a lack of preparation. Your routine becomes your trading base.

## Record-keeping and Trade Journal

Detailed trade journaling exposes patterns in your trading results. Each trade entry should specify the setup type, market conditions, entry reason, and outcome. My personal notebooks assisted in determining which price action patterns were most effective under various scenarios.

A single GBPJPY trade journal post revealed an important pattern in my trading. After examining months of trades, I discovered that my biggest win rate came from specific price action setups during the London-New York session overlap.

## Performance Analysis

A regular performance evaluation identifies strengths and faults in your trading strategy.

Through a thorough review of my trades, I learnt that certain price action patterns performed better in trending markets than in range conditions. This knowledge greatly enhanced my trade selection.

Trading AUDUSD revealed significant patterns in my performance data. Pin bar rejections at critical levels resulted in more successful trades than breakouts. This analysis resulted in strategy refinements that increased overall profitability.

## Common Mistakes To Avoid

Experience taught me valuable lessons regarding common trading blunders. Trader failures are frequently caused by overtrading during range markets, neglecting trade market context, and using inadequate position sizing. Understanding these hazards will help you avoid them.

My early USDJPY trades revealed some frequent errors. Taking trades without obvious price action confirmation resulted in avoidable losses. Learning from these mistakes greatly enhanced my trading discipline.

## Psychology & Discipline

Trading psychology frequently influences success and failure. The ability to stick to your plan despite emotional demands makes all the difference. Through years of trading, I've learnt that emotional control is more important than technical analysis.

Maintaining discipline in turbulent EURUSD sessions proved difficult. Strong price swings encouraged deviation from scheduled entrances and exits. Keeping to set norms safeguarded my capital throughout these stressful times.

## Strategy Testing and Validation

Testing your strategy carefully instills trust in your approach. Back-testing price action patterns allows us to better grasp their reliability. Based on my experience, tested techniques outperform untested ones under pressure.

Testing GBPUSD price action techniques provided useful insights. Certain patterns demonstrated greater reliability in various market scenarios. This insight aided trade selection and risk management decisions.

## Adapting to Market Change

Markets change continually, necessitating strategy modification. Your plan must include instructions for responding to changing circumstances.

Throughout market cycles, I've learnt that flexibility under set norms ensures profitability.

Trading across market phases demonstrated the importance of strategy modification. Ranging market strategies failed during trending periods. Understanding when to change your strategy helps you avoid big drawdowns.

## Risk Management Framework

Comprehensive risk management safeguards your trading capital. Beyond basic position sizing, your plan must account for correlation risk, market condition risk, and overall exposure. My institutional experience emphasised the importance of multi-layered risk management.

Managing several EURUSD positions educated me about exposure risk.

Correlated roles required smaller position sizes to maintain acceptable total risk levels. This understanding helped to prevent overleveraging during large market movements.

## The Road to Consistency

Consistent outcomes need time and commitment to your plan. Small, consistent profits accumulate to large profits over time. My trading experience demonstrated that consistency stems from rigorous plan execution rather than seeking massive individual trades.

This chapter's themes provide a foundation for long-term trading success. In the next chapter, we'll look at advanced mastery principles that expand on this foundation. Developing and adhering to a thorough plan is critical to your trading performance.

When you apply these planning principles, your trading evolution accelerates. They provide the structure required for constant profitability and good risk management.

# Chapter 9

## Advanced Price Action Mastery

**Combining Multiple Patterns**

The full force of price action occurs when multiple patterns coincide. Through my institutional trading experience, I've noticed that pattern combinations result in the highest probability setups. These convergences frequently predict large market movements before they occur.

Trading the EURUSD demonstrated how pattern combinations work in real markets.

One of my most winning trades came from a pin bar that formed within a broader engulfing pattern at a major resistance level. The alignment of these patterns considerably increased the power of the signal.

## Complex price action setups

Complex arrangements necessitate a thorough understanding of market structure. These advanced formations incorporate multiple price action variables as well as certain market conditions. My trading records suggest that difficult setups, albeit rare, frequently result in higher profits.

A GBPJPY configuration demonstrated this flawlessly. The formation included a false break, multiple inside bars, and a reversal pattern near a significant support level. Understanding how these elements interacted resulted in capturing a 400-pip move.

## Order Flow Analysis

Order flow manifests itself as certain price action patterns. Large institutional orders leave different fingerprints in price fluctuation. My years on the trading desk taught me how to see these patterns and trade alongside the smart money.

Trading USDJPY revealed apparent order flow patterns. A series of bull candles with falling top wicks indicated sequential buying pressure and institutional accumulation. This understanding assisted in timed entries for maximum effectiveness.

## Institutional Trading Levels:

Major institutions prioritise specific price levels. When these levels are approached, unique price action patterns emerge.

I've learnt from experience that institutional action frequently clusters around round numbers and major technical levels.

During one of my AUDUSD trades, I observed sustained institutional activity near the 0.7500 level. The price action displayed conventional accumulation and distribution patterns. Understanding these patterns led to fantastic trading opportunities.

**Advanced Entry Techniques**.

Refined entry methods considerably enhance trade execution performance. Beyond basic pattern detection, advanced entries include multiple timeframe analysis and price action triggers. My trading really improved after mastering these tactics.

One EURGBP trade demonstrated advanced entry techniques. Instead of entering soon after pattern completion, waiting for smaller timeframe confirmation increased the entry price significantly. This technique lowered risk while preserving profit possibilities.

Professional price action interpretation requires understanding market environment. Each pattern has a distinct meaning based on market conditions. Through years of trading, I've learnt that context is often more important than the pattern.

The trading of USDCAD effectively showed this principle. Because of the broader market situation, an engulfing pattern that would normally signify a reversal showed continuation. This understanding precluded taking a counter-trend stance.

## Pattern Evolution and Adaptation

Price action patterns shift as markets change. What worked last year may need to be adjusted today. My experience has shown that effective traders regularly adjust their pattern detection to current market conditions.

During moments of extreme volatility, customary patterns have to be modified. Wider pauses and alternative confirmation criteria became essential. Adapting to these modifications ensured profitability during difficult times.

## Advanced Risk Management.

Sophisticated risk management takes into account multiple elements. Aside from simple stop placement, advanced traders consider market volatility, correlation risk, and pattern consistency. My institutional background emphasised the value of comprehensive risk assessment.

Managing multiple EURUSD trades taught me excellent risk management lessons. Correlated patterns necessitated smaller position sizes in order to maintain acceptable portfolio risk. This understanding prevented overexposure during major market movements.

## Market microstructure analysis

Understanding the market microstructure improves price action trading. Bid-ask spreads, market depth, and order flow offer context to pattern analysis. My experience has shown that microstructure awareness increases trade timing greatly.

GBPUSD trading during liquid hours exhibited significant microstructure patterns. Spread behaviour and order flow offered more evidence for price action indications. This extensive analysis enhanced trade execution and profitability.

# The Path of Mastery

Mastering price action requires attention and experience. Each market has distinct difficulties and opportunities. by years of trading, I've learnt that mastery is achieved by continuous learning and adaptation.

The notions presented in this chapter are advanced price action trading principles. In the last chapter, we'll look at how these concepts are applied in the actual world. Your trading performance is dependent on incorporating these advanced concepts into your current technique.

Understanding and applying these sophisticated principles will expedite your progress as a master trader. They provide the advantage required for consistent success in competitive markets.

# Chapter 10

## Real-World Applications

**Live Trading Examples**

The main test of price action trading occurs in actual market conditions. Through thousands of trades, I've seen how theoretical knowledge is translated into practical results. Each trade provides its own set of problems that put your understanding and discipline to the test.

During a tumultuous EURUSD session, the ideal price action situation materialised. A pin bar formed at a critical support level during the London Open.

The context indicated oversold conditions with diminishing selling pressure. Taking this trade required confidence in both the setup and market reading abilities.

## Case Studies for Successful Trades

Success leaves traces in the form of recurring patterns. My most lucrative GBPJPY trade demonstrated ideal price action confluence. Multiple timeframe analysis revealed pattern alignment, and market context backed the trade direction.

The trade began with the daily pin bar at resistance. Four-hour charts displayed a complex consolidation pattern, whilst one-hour charts showed strong signals of buying pressure. This multi-layered confirmation resulted in a big profit when the price moved as expected.

## Common Scenarios and Solutions

Market scenarios occur with amazing consistency. Throughout my years of institutional trading, I have met numerous such instances. Each case necessitates unique tactics depending on price action cues.

Trading AUDUSD in range conditions gave me vital lessons. When prices approached range boundaries, certain candlestick patterns indicated possible reversals. Understanding these scenarios aided in the development of consistent trading strategies for varying market conditions.

## Adapting to Market Change

Markets change continually, necessitating strategy modification.

Your approach must adapt to market conditions while keeping key principles. In my experience, structural flexibility leads to consistent profitability.

During the 2020 volatility increase, typical price action patterns need change. Wider pauses and more stringent confirmation requirements became essential. Adapting to these developments while upholding fundamental price action principles safeguarded capital under difficult conditions.

## Building Long-Term Consistency.

Consistency develops from the careful application of established principles. Small, consistent earnings compound into huge returns, as I've discovered on my trading journey. Focussing on the process rather than the outcome leads to long-term success.

Trading USDJPY taught me about consistency. Instead of looking for big winners, taking little profits from apparent price action setups proved more consistent. This method resulted in consistent account growth while minimising risk.

## Creating Your Trading Edge

Your advantage stems from your remarkable pattern detection abilities. Each trader gains skill in particular settings and market conditions. My advantage came from specialising in reversal patterns at critical technical levels.

One EURGBP trade exhibited this specialised expertise. While others witnessed random price movements, I noticed a sophisticated reversal pattern emerging at a crucial support level. This specialised understanding resulted in tremendous economic possibilities.

## Real Market Challenges

Live markets pose unanticipated obstacles. Years of trading have tested my strategy and discipline. Overcoming these hurdles boosted my trading strategy.

Trading USDCAD during news releases demonstrated how price action responds to volatility. Quick pattern creation and resolution necessitated rapid decision-making while preserving analytical rigour. These experiences helped me improve my ability to read market conditions accurately.

## Risk Management in Practice

Practical risk management frequently differs from theory. Actual market conditions necessitate swift modifications and prompt action. My institutional experience emphasised the value of dynamic risk management.

Managing several GBPUSD positions shows practical risk management. Correlation between places necessitated smaller sizes and close monitoring. This real-world implementation of risk management principles successfully protected trading funds.

## The Journey to Proficiency

Becoming skilled necessitates ongoing learning and adaptability. Each trade offers opportunities for advancement and progress. I've witnessed how theoretical knowledge may be transformed into practical skill via years of market involvement.

The concepts taught in this book provide the cornerstone for successful price action trading. Understanding these principles is the first step on your journey, but practical application and tenacious study are what will get you there.

Your trader development never fully ends. Markets are constantly shifting, bringing new difficulties and possibilities. Accept this journey of continual improvement and adaptation.

# Conclusion

This book has taken us on a journey through the complex realm of price action trading. My journey from a struggling indicator-dependent trader to a successful price action specialist has lasted over fifteen years, and I've shared the most significant lessons from this experience.

Trading altered my entire outlook on markets. During my early days at the London trading desk, I observed millions of dollars travel through the markets on a daily basis. However, the most important lesson came from seeing how price movement alone revealed the entire tale of market attitude and direction.

The efficacy of price action trading stems from its simplicity and directness. You do not need complex indicators or advanced algorithms to trade profitably. The raw price movement gives all of the required information. I learnt this lesson the hard way, spending years overcomplicating my strategy before realising the simplicity of basic price action.

Your success in price action trading is dependent on understanding fundamental principles. Understanding candlestick patterns, market structure, and trading psychology is the foundation. I've shared how these variables interact in this book to generate winning trading opportunities.

The strategies and concepts taught are not simply theoretical; they have been battle-tested in many trades. Every technique, from the fundamental pin bar layout to complicated multiple pattern combinations, is based on real-world market experience. I've seen these patterns work successfully across a variety of currency pairs and market circumstances.

In price action trading, market psychology is essential. The patterns we see reflect the aggregate activity of all market players. Understanding this psychology allows you to predict future market movements. I've learnt through years of institutional trading how major players leave footprints in price action.

Risk management is the cornerstone of trading success. No plan works without proper risk management. The methods shared in this book emphasise both capital preservation and profit development. My own trading success occurred only after I learnt risk management principles.

Trading demands ongoing adaptation. Markets change, and effective traders must develop alongside them.

The principles of price action remain constant, but their application must be adjusted according to market conditions. This agility distinguishes successful traders from those who struggle.

There will be hurdles on your trading journey. Every successful trader faces hurdles along the way. The idea is to maintain discipline and trust your price action analysis. My personal path had many obstacles, but each one taught me significant lessons about how to grow.

The real-world experiences shared in this book show how theory becomes practice. From precise trade setups to management choices, these examples demonstrate price action trading in action. They are based on real-world scenarios that you may meet along your trading journey.

Remember that profitability is achieved via the persistent application of proven principles.

Before moving on to more advanced strategies, make sure you understand the fundamentals. Rather than chasing novel settings, I found that trading straightforward, well-understood patterns produced the most profitable results.

Patience and dedication are required to advance as a price action trader. Your success is dependent on real application and experience, but the concepts shared here lay the groundwork. Take the time to research market behaviour and practise pattern recognition.

The journey does not end with finishing this book. Markets continuously provide fresh learning opportunities. Maintain your curiosity, discipline, and trust in your analysis. Continuous improvement and adaptation are key to trading success.

Price action trading provides a path to steady profit for those who are ready to learn its principles.

Your road map is provided by the strategies, insights, and experiences shared in this book. The rest is up to your dedication to understanding and applying these concepts.

Your trading future is in your control. Use the information presented here as a foundation, but create your own trading approach. You will learn which tactics work best for you via experience and application.

The market awaits your participation. With your price action trading expertise, you're ready to start your journey to trading success. Trust the process, stay disciplined, and allow price action to lead your trading decisions.

Remember that all great traders began as beginners. Understanding and applying these essential principles is the first step on your path to mastery. The journey may be difficult, but the benefits are well worth the effort.

## Video Access Page

Thank you for purchasing my book! As a token of my appreciation, I've made available exclusive video content just for you.

To access your complimentary videos, simply visit:

https://mega.nz/folder/IYZRQZTL#UIoA3WK6Gb_OfS2Xxq-iRA

Thank you for your support, and I hope these additional resources enhance your reading experience!

Best regards,

**James willy**

www.ingramcontent.com/pod-product-compliance
Lightning Source LLC
Chambersburg PA
CBHW071036240526
45469CB00006BD/2233